WHEN WE WERE YOUNG

A Collection Of Unapologetic Poetry

ALANNA RUSNAK

Originally released as an ebook in 2013
ASIN B00F3QNT9A

First Printing: 2018
ALANNA RUSNAK PUBLISHING

ISBN 13: 978-17752792-4-2
ISBN 10: 1775279243

Alanna Rusnak Publishing
282906 Normanby/Bentinck Townline
Durham, Ontario, Canada, N0G 1R0
www.publishing.alannarusnak.com

Contact publisher for Library and Archives Catalogue information

Cover design by Alanna Rusnak
Photography courtesy of pixabay.com

for the dreamers

Contents

When We Were Young
A Collection Of Unapologetic Poetry

Alanna Rusnak

2018

I Would Like To Have Been

I would like to have been
a nineteenth century poet
with thees and thous
and other wonders

I will not be

I was born in 1979

A Conversation

Eternity approached a lazy man and asked of him, "Why?"
And he said,
    "The sky is raw and I am soft.
    Please be my original drug;
    Draw me true and read me wild -
    Like fiery spring art or sweet summer metaphors.
    Picture me as white tongues of bare need,
       dreaming of delicate rain behind chiseled sculptures.
    Could you mould winter of young wood?
       or compose symphonies with colour?
    Could you create rhythm with light
       or language of dust?"
And she replied,
    "I would piece frantic moments into a still-life garden
    beneath an emotionally rich and monumental flood.
    I am water;
       swim and live."

Alanna Rusnak

Ode To A Loney Nun

A praying mantis is kneeling
before the altar of poverty;
her habit in a knot.

Lipstick lies
a melted disaster in her pocket;
she wears it only at night in her cell
with her crucifix and the Virgin Mary.

She carries the child she never had in her heart
there beside the Jack of Spades,
of Hearts,
of Daniels.

Holy mother, convent goddess;
I don't envy you your piety, your calling
even your [un]fashionable attire.
I do admire you your courage and your devotion.

Do you ever go barefoot
just to feel the cool tiles on your soul?
Even when no one is looking?

God bless you.

Maybe you could ask him to do the same for me.

Warm Like May

Winter beats against my memories of you
but you are warm like May;
like sun-bleached sand
beneath naked toes.

Alanna Rusnak

The Preacher

The preacher has a silver agenda
behind the pulpit with his anti-devilism.
"THOU SHALT NOT SIN!"
But I've heard him yell at his twelve-year-old son.
They have cursed upon the foyer of
the holy of holies.

He talks of disciples and gates
and golden streets and miracles
and I'm too embarrassed to admit
that the idea of heaven
terrifies me.

My Name Isn't Samson

A small boy [child]
once asked me
if I could help him
tear down the walls
that were rooted
so solidly
in his
father's foundation.
I smiled
and kissed his hair
-gently-
and said,
"My name
isn't Samson."

There You Are

There you are
sitting in all your perfection
[of lack there of]
spitting judgment down my throat.
I felt your envy
against my neck
so I vomited on your kitchen floor.
Serves you right, mister.

You make me proud to be better than you.

How Shall You Paint Me?

How then shall you paint me?
Will it be like Michael Angelo?
Or Picasso?
Either is fine.
I feel no preference.
Just a burning need for colour.

Chained

chained
here we sit
writing with the frozen breath
of immortal perfection

gentle reflection
touches me
where I am broken

come sweet diffusion
enter with care and hostility

war times
and
bad times
and
sexuality
and everywhere
in between

Please Go Away

If I were not myself
I would let you love me
in a thirty-three dollar motel
with dirty carpet and orange curtains
that hang like dead hair.

If I were not myself
I would let you stretch me
between the moon and a rusted Chevrolet

If I were not myself
I would let you kiss me
as if we'd always done it this way.

If I were not myself
I would be a slut for you;
your concubine of passion and misdirection.

If I were not myself...

But I am.

Please go away.

I would not want to want you.
I am quite pleased with my life without you.
I don't need a beautiful John Doe
spouting lines in my ear
to feel like I'm worth anything more
than a quickie and a Happy Meal.

Please go away.

For an extra twenty-five cents
you may enjoy my rejection
with a side of pickles
if that would make it easier to swallow.

Please go away.

I Would Like To Make You Cry

I would like to make you cry;
purging salt
to unmask your demon
and make you real enough to love.

Who made you the jester?
The idiot?
The procrastinator?

Who made you beautiful?

Here is my demon.
He is ugly and breathtaking and all the reasons
you want to touch my flesh to see if I'm still breathing.

There is a light in your window...

[I saw your face - just like John Lennon said I would
before he died.]

...I turned mine out hours ago.

It was cold without you here tonight.
Queen Mab has written an insufferable story
for my R.E.M.

Sleep soundly.
Please cry.

Alanna Rusnak

You Hang Your Laundry

You hang your laundry
as if it were an art display
like it was something beautiful;
a linen chime to make music
with the wind in the trees.

Undo The Unstrung Hero

undo the unstrung hero
white horse
black horse
afro...
benevolent charm on the riverbed
self-suppressed resistance
resisting time
in a cardboard box
of paper angels
and broken wings
and unstrung heroes

For Hitler

silver-lined summer-salt
on clouds with moulded lashes
and pleistocene dragons
you kick the world
with a goal total oppression
you rip the page slowly
so as not to scar the art
you break me
with sticks and stones
and capture my naiveté
in a foggy bottle of
unsurpassed glory and fame
make me an instrument
of your callous undoing
as you throw me
like crusted mud
out the second story window

I am a Paintbrush

I am a paintbrush,
poised above the riverbed
of luxury and creativity.
I am thought.
I am thoughtless.

I am the wind.

Alanna Rusnak

The Temples

The temples of nature and neglect
awaken from a nightmare
into a strange world
of treasure
and souls of mystery.

The threatened ways
of the people
promise a web of evidence
stretching around the world:
this foreign land of conquest.

The amazing testimony of the sea -
that walk on water
to an old storehouse
of ancient generations
and fair winds
that could knock you down
on your way up.

Fresh clues find enough
desert in the sands
for new light and
a humble life
without luxury.

Clarity Of Harmony

Shadows shake beneath a moment of your vision;
behind this symphony of fast sweet dreams
I could go mad with wanting your beauty
to flood me where I am.

    Sing sad fiddle...
      Scream bitter wind...
        Lie softly love...

I would swim in the light of your power if
it would let me taste the water of your music.

I Am No Less Than Yours

You are perfect in your imperfection
with paper wings that have graced heaven
more than once and a melody so calm and wicked
from your baby blues that it might break me
if I stare too long.

I would that you were the ocean
and I could let your waves
kiss the tension from my weary feet
or the travel from my legs.

In my disgust I am beautiful to you
and you terrify me.

And who am I?

I am no less than yours.

Empty Your Thoughts

Empty your thoughts
unto my nakedness;
Cling to the iron railing
-discretion equals pride-
Bind me with ropes of empty indifference
and stand by
as I drain my life
into a bottle
for your collection.

Alanna Rusnak

Made In Taiwan

Who am I?
I am she.
Possibly a bit of he.
Definitely something more than them.
(I hope.)
I have done things of merit.
I have said things of merit.
I have made things of merit.

But I am terrified that if you turned me over
there would be a stamp on my soul
that reads, "MADE IN TAIWAN"
and I would be nothing more than
a plastic doll
being posed through the motions
of sit-com crap
that Barbara Walters
has the audacity to call
real life.

You Were My Instrument Of Joy

You were my instrument of joy;
robbing the wild sky of blue,
of red,
of sleepy art -
wasting no thoughts
on angry goddesses
or empty gifts.

You suffer for balance
knowing that only harmony
demands easy dreaming.

So, come as you would;
we are still falling from winter
and drunk on cool rain.

In this bare forest
there is life and smell and flood.
And you are screaming
behind the sculpted garden beds.
So distant
and frighteningly transparent,
and not at all who I thought you were.

I Will Be Yours

I will be yours always.
This I will not
hesitate to promise.
A guarantee signed
in my own blood
if you need that security.
If anyone should challenge that
you need only
to hold me to the light
and they will see
your watermark upon me.

Love Me Like Mad

Love me like mad and I will be yours always;
for an eternity of pounding lights
and summer storms.

The sky of your raw stare
robs me of my lazy lies and dreamy needs
and I rock to the time of your delirious beauty
from this hot shadow road.

Elaboration [Velveteen Rabbit]

Super-hero action figure;
 poised,
daring the battle,
strong and tolerant
until the house starts to burn...

That's when the skin horse whispers,
"You're not real."

Arson Poetry

I would like to
light the sky on fire
and dance
a naive tango
against
my arson poetry

Here I Sing

here I sing with my pen
rather than my voice
against the orchestrated silence
of human passion
here I whisper
an aria of secret thoughts
and private musings
here I am
exposed to the masses
and suddenly
I feel so small
like maybe I am
nothing more than
a faint reflection
in a café window
with hand-painted advertisements
for grandé cappuccino's
and home-baked pies

Trudge Through Summer Storms

You trudge through summer storms
beneath smooth, hot skies.

You read dreams and dance
as if this were your final symphony.

You chain your inhibitions
to a thousand rocks.

You let the rain rust their power
and turn it into a pile of red dust
for you to sprinkle on your eggs
like paprika.

You Stop Me Like Iron

You stop me like iron
hot and screaming;
You're drunk
and manipulated by lazy skies
and red meat and live TV.

I am sad to see you
beneath frantic fingers -
beating out a delicate rhythm
in a whisper of a gown,
your wet hair clinging
to his watery skin.

In your bed there is
a moment of music
though I think you are too weak
and so all you hear
is the stillness
and all you smell
is his sweat.

Through Surreal Rhythms

you appear
through surreal rhythms
and whisper
with the electric passion
of angels and moments
far above fashion
or impression
and I imagine
your bold chisel
loving me into someone
absurd and beautiful

Behind This Smooth Blue Stare

I ache behind this smooth blue stare
Not for you in your felt-skin, deliriously pleasing
Not for a thousand tongues to whisper of my beauty
But for life to have vision
And the music to be less bare.

Through the shimmer of rosewater
I could recall your light
Though the winter is dark
And the garden has seen much death.

Dear Flower Child

Beautiful flower child
let me touch your hand
and get a sense of the magic
of your too short/long [?] existence.

Take me back, Mr. Time Machine
to Anti-Vietnam America
and I'll kiss the first twenty boys I see.

You Look At Me

You look at me
through your self-pity
and Hebraic window pains
and I giggle over
your three dollar hair cut
and thrift store sneakers
as you run from the
cruelty of my judgement.

Forgive me my
personally defined
sense of worth
and I'll forgive you
the Wrangler jeans
with ink doodles on the thigh.

Your Skin Is Hot

Your skin is hot like summer petals
and you whisper smooth secrets
as I sleep against your hair.

Let's be lazy.
Let's fall into each other and drown
beneath a glimpse of bare eternity.

You can be my lover
and I will be your goddess
in a shallow gown
of water and good intentions.

I Wanted To Make Love To You Today

I wanted to maké love to you today
...with words...
You are the most beautiful creature
I've seen all summer -
Hunched like Quasi
with the face of a curious little boy
riding the chaos in a state of grace.

You may write of love and sex
and women and purity
and the consumption of a hostile crowd
but your crooked smile seems genuine
and I like to think you love me
...with words...

I Sit Here Tonight

I sit here tonight upon this preposition
in a dimness that allows me to see with my mind's eye.
There is magic in my fingers;
I feel it there, reminding me of you.
I can take myself anywhere
to Paris or New York City
and even there, among the romance
of bouquets and theatres
and unrealistic picture shows
I find it impossible not to love you.

This is my whole heart.
I will take it with me everywhere.
You

　　　　　...are my heart.

For The Boy Who Called Me Impeccable In 1997

"good day, sir - what is my fortune?"
and you would flash me your signature
gothic [endearing] grin and look over your
tarot cards and I would stand there believing
that you believed in them with all your being
and that passion amazed and frightened me -
then you would write on some scrap that
my fashion sense was impeccable and how
you enjoyed my poetry so much and I thought
that if this wasn't 1997 I might have loved you
though I wasn't sure what impeccable meant -
what a shame we barely spoke before june

I Want To Remember You Forever

I want to remember you forever as you are right now;
perfect and innocent and beautiful and mine.

Let Me Catch The Tear

Let me catch the tear from
your heart before it shatters

IMMORTAL

like a chicken bone in the desert

Sahara-hot with blood
wanting what cannot be had

You see me and my love
and pink vomit
against a watered-down background
of pinecones and needles and anesthetic

Knock out on the dock
Plastic harbor in the bathtub
No bubbles -
they make you sick

You stopped smiling and closed the door

Thoughts On My Mother

This is your most beautiful moment
standing in a room of semi-darkness
my baby help against your warmth
hushing and singing and loving
so that I might stop crying
and go to bed

Alanna Rusnak

Touch Me Again

Touch me again and let me fall again
into a sea of masculinity.
Kiss me with intense tongues of fire.
Want me in the way of a man;
with unforgiving lust and sexuality.
Quench this lingering thirst
with wild abandon.
Satisfy me and you and us
lying naked on the kitchen floor.

I Am

I am soft
I am stone
I am sweet
I am sour
I am beautiful
I am ugly
I am music
I am silence
I am poetry
I am shadow
I am kind
I am cold
I am lovely
I am a storm
I am complex
I am simple
I am breathing
I am breathtaking
I am summer
I am winter
I am a moment
I am forever

I am youth

I tried to wrap my arms around the world
but the sky got in the way

I Remember Yours

The moon hangs his shadow against your nudity.
It is summer.
It is hot.
Do you remember my name?
I remember yours.
I remember you.
Bastard!
I hate winter!

Those Long Nights

I created you for those long nights
when love seemed impossible;
as if menopause-extreme-is hidden
in the non-existent grey hairs.
Sweet mother love, gently unfold the bloody mass
of womb and tissue - child unborn.

Breathless

Death is an echo.

An echo.

I created you; friend, enemy, lover
to molest my brain with your tentacles
and reassure me that tomorrow
nothing will have changed
and life will live continuous
even though reincarnation
was invented by a dead man.

Show Me Your Weakness

Show me your weakness and I will be yours always;
speaking to you in a language we understand
only through our love.

Let's dream here from our golden ship
and float away to satin beds
and pounding symphonies within our heads.

Woodstock Remembered (Though I Don't)

the moon creates honest shadows
against the windows of insubordination
this glorious union of nude bodies
and lovemaking
beautiful
in makeshift shelters of skin and poetry
designs advanced freedom and pregnancy
one mouth whispers
'I love you'
in forty ears
in return for satisfaction forty times over

I am a foreign virgin amidst hippie nymphos

kiss me softly in the twilight of your wings

Alanna Rusnak

This Is Not The End

This is not the end so wipe the tears from your eyes
glowing in the dark
celebrate every tomorrow with poetry
fresh and ancient
and remember my face
saying see you later
and not goodbye

ABOUT THE AUTHOR

Alanna Rusnak lives on a small patch of untameable land in mid-western Ontario with her three children, husband, and an over-weight cat. Fuelled by copious amounts of caffeine and chocolate, she writes fiction and creative non-fiction from within her tiny study.

Facebook *facebook.com/alannarusnakauthor*
Goodreads *goodreads.com/alannarusnak*
Instagram *@alannarusnak*
Twitter *@alannarusnak*

Subscribe for updates at **alannarusnak.com** for news of upcoming releases, press events, and the status of various projects.

If you've enjoyed this, or other books by Alanna, please consider leaving a review anywhere her books are sold or promoted . (Amazon, Goodreads, Barnes & Noble, Chapters Indigo, etc.)

Also by Alanna Rusnak

Eve Undone (2016)

Kissing Johnny (2016)

The Church in the Wildwood (2017)

Just Words Volume 1 (contributing author) (2017)

The Ghost of Iris Carver (2018)

and coming soon

Black Bird

.

www.ingramcontent.com/pod-product-compliance
Lightning Source LLC
Chambersburg PA
CBHW060723030426
42337CB00017B/2987